# Dog Food Recipes

# For

# Kidney and Heart Health

## By Rupert C. Robertson III

*This book is dedicated to*
*Tessa (Chenal Contessa Celtic Corgi),*
*our twelve year old Corgi*
*who is struggling with kidney disease,*
*and*
*to Judy,*
*our twelve year old hound*
*who is struggling with heart disease.*

# Table of Contents

Rice, Sweet Potato and Meat

Beef and Rice

Meat and Cereal

Chicken, Egg and Rice

Homecooked for Kidney Disease/ Failure

Kidney Healing Recipe

Egg & Potato Diet

Chicken and Potato diet

Rice, Beef and Egg Diet

Canine Restricted Protein Diet

Beef and Tapioca Diet

Egg Whites and Tapioca Diet

Chicken and Tapioca Diet

Eggs and Rice Diet

Egg Whites and Rice Diet

## Heart Healthy Recipes

For fish lovers

Beef, Potato and Chicken Fat Diet

Beef and Potato Diet

Chicken, Potato and Chicken Fat Diet

Beef, Rice and Chicken Fat Diet

Beef and Rice Diet

Chicken, Rice and Chicken Fat Diet

Chicken and Rice Diet

Seafood delight

"Russian Bim"

Shaoping chicken

Veggie lamb

Beef and Potato Diet

Chicken and Potato Diet

Beef and Rice Diet

Chicken and Rice Diet

Heart Healthy Chicken

## Healthy Treats

Turkey Dog Treats

From Thrifty Fun

Ingredients:

Directions:

Albi's Treats

Peanut Butter Cookies

Chicken Jerky

Fruit and Vegetable Strips

# Introduction

First, let me state for the record, I am not a veterinarian. I have simply done extensive research to try and find out how to help older and ailing dogs and cats. Over the years, my wife and I have adopted rescue and abandoned dogs and cats. We have watched them struggle with various conditions as they grew older and have searched for ways to prolong their lives without making them suffer. It is difficult, and often very expensive, to find a diet that will help them survive some of the problems associated with aging or kidney, heart and other serious problems.

The recipes that are included in this work are a compilation of the research that we have done to help our own four-legged family members. I hope it is helpful to you. If you mass produce these recipes, you will find that most of them can be done for the same cost (or less) as lower priced canned dog food. They are far less expensive than prescription dog food and better for them, since there are no added preservatives, dyes, flavor enhancers or other unwanted chemicals. This cost does not include labor but, since it is a labor of love, it shouldn't. The reward of seeing your pet healthier is enough to offset the cost of labor.

You will notice that there is some conflict when recipes include onions and garlic. Different experts have different opinions and I am not in a position to advise in either direction. I personally include very limited amounts of onion in my personal recipes but do not add in garlic. After a lot of searching, I can't state, for good or bad, that garlic or onions have a place in dog foods. I would check with my vet and see what they think. I would also ask what they base their opinion on.

I have tried to credit all of my sources for these recipes so that you can further research their ideas and credentials. Many are veterinarians and health care professionals, but some are people like you and me that have simply done a lot of research and come up with their own recipe. Please, feel free to share any of them with your friends or your local animal shelter. It may help someone's best friend.

# What Not To Feed Your Dog

The list of the following foods, obtained from the Humane Society, may be dangerous to your pet. Please do not feed any of them to your dog if you want to keep it healthy. *

- Alcoholic beverages
- Apple seeds
- Apricot pits
- Avocados
- Cherry pits
- Candy (particularly chocolate—which is toxic to dogs, cats, and ferrets—and any candy containing the toxic sweetener Xylitol)
- Coffee (grounds, beans, and chocolate-covered espresso beans)
- *Garlic or onions
- Grapes
- Gum (can cause blockages and sugar free gums may contain the toxic sweetener Xylitol)
- Hops (used in home beer brewing)
- Macadamia nuts
- Moldy foods

Mushroom plants

Mustard seeds

Onions and onion powder

Peach pits

Potato leaves and stems (green parts)

Raisins

Rhubarb leaves

Salt

Tea (because it contains caffeine)

Tomato leaves and stems (green parts)

Walnuts

Xylitol (artificial sweetener that is toxic to pets)

Yeast dough

*Garlic and onions have mixed reviews from veterinarians. Please come to your own conclusions.

# Kidney Healthy Recipes

## Homemade Diet Recipes for Dogs With Kidney Disease

For dogs that suffer from kidney disease, a proper diet is vital in order to slow the progression of the disease and to prevent toxins from building-up in the pet's system. With some dogs, getting them to eat a commercial renal-support diet can be a challenge, plus many veterinarians advise against it. Also, in many cases, the cost of such foods can be prohibitive to some owners. If you are inclined to cook for your dog, here are some excellent recipes that can be used as substitutes for commercial prescription diets. We recommend preparing your dog's meals yourself from fresh whole, organic (if possible) foods at home. Recipes can be made in large batches and frozen in meal sized portions to avoid having to cook or prepare meals from scratch each day. Simply adjust the amount of food proportionally based on your dog's weight and store in meal sized bags.

Note:

Some recipes call for dog greens. Dog greens are commercially prepared and contain ingredients such as: SPIRULINA, CHLORELLA, ALFALFA, BARLEY GRASS, WHEAT GRASS, KELP & IRISH MOSS

I could not find a recipe for home-made dog greens but they can be purchased at almost any pet store or on-line if you choose a recipe that includes them as an ingredient.

## Egg & Sweet Potato

This recipe, from Five Leaf Pet Pharmacy, is the daily amount for a 40 lb dog, divide into as many serving as you wish. Adjust recipe according to your dog's weight.

Two large boiled Organic Eggs
3 cups of boiled Organic Sweet Potatoes with skin
1 1/2 cups of pureed or shredded Organic Vegetables – Carrots, Broccoli, Cucumbers, Tomatoes, Leafy Greens, Parsley etc
1 tablespoon of Organic Oil blend – any organic oil blend that says 3-6-9 omegas preferable with DHA, UDO's makes a very nice one.
Dog Greens

## Beef & Rice

This recipe has been adapted from Dr. Pitcairn's New Complete Guide to Natural Health for Dogs and Cats

This is one day of food for a 40 lb dog. Adjust recipe according to your dog's weight.

1/4 pound (1/2 cup) regular fat Hamburger/Ground Beef, Chicken, Turkey or Lamb (preferably organic, you can have the butcher grind some organic meat for you)
2 3/4 cups cooked Organic White Rice
2 large Organic Eggs
1/4 cup cooked Organic Carrots
2 Tablespoons Organic Safflower Oil
2 Tablespoons fresh diced Parsley
*1/2 clove Garlic (if he likes it)

Mix all ingredients together and serve raw if the dog will accept it. Otherwise bake for approximately 20 minutes in the oven at 350F, let cool then add Dog Greens to each meal before serving.

http://dogcathomeprepareddiet.com/diet_and_chronic_renal_disease.html

## Eggs and Potato

Low Protein, Low phosphorus, High Potassium, Normal Sodium

1 cooked whole egg, chicken
3 cups potatoes boiled in skin (369 grams)
1 tablespoon chicken fat (14 grams)
1 1/2 calcium carbonate tablets (600 mg calcium)
1/2 multiple vitamin-mineral tablet

provides 600 kcalories, 15.1 g protein, 18.5 g fat
supports caloric needs of 18 pound dog
provides phosphorus 53%, potassium 322%, sodium 114% of a dog's daily needs.
To feed this diet with a normal amount of phosphorus substitute 2.5 grams bone meal powder for the 1 1/2 calcium carbonate tablets

http://dogcathomepreppareddiet.com/diet_and_chronic_renal_disease.html

## Beef and Potato

Low Protein, Low phosphorus, High Potassium, Low Sodium

2 ounces (raw weight) lean ground beef, cooked (57 grams)
3 cups potatoes boiled in skin (369 grams)
2 tablespoons chicken fat (28 grams)
1 1/2 calcium carbonate tablets (600 mg calcium)
1/2 multiple vitamin-mineral tablet

provides 737 kcalories, 18.6 g protein, 32.5 g fat
supports caloric needs of 23 to 24 pound dog
provides phosphorus 43%, potassium 293%, sodium 54%
of a dog's daily needs.
To feed this diet with a normal amount of phosphorus
substitute 3 grams bone meal powder for the 1 1/2
calcium carbonate tablets

http://dogcathomeprepareddiet.com/diet_and_chronic_renal_disease.html

## Eggs and Tapioca

Low Protein, Low phosphorus, Low Potassium, Normal Sodium

3 cooked whole eggs, chicken
2 cups tapioca, cooked, (125 g dry before cooking)
1 tablespoon chicken fat (14 grams)
1 1/2 calcium carbonate tablets (600 mg calcium)
1/2 multiple vitamin-mineral tablet

provides 779 kcalories, 19.3 g protein, 28.9 g fat
supports caloric needs of 25 pound dog
provides phosphorus 40%, potassium 30%, sodium 216% of a dog's daily needs.
To feed this diet with a normal amount of phosphorus substitute 3 grams bone meal powder for the 1 1/2 calcium carbonate tablets

http://dogcathomeprepareddiet.com/diet_and_chronic_renal_disease.html

## Beef and Tapioca

Low Protein, Low phosphorus, Low Potassium, Low Sodium

4 ounces (raw weight) lean ground beef, cooked (114 grams)
2 cups tapioca, cooked, (125 g dry before cooking)
2 tablespoons chicken fat (28 grams)
1 1/2 calcium carbonate tablets (600 mg calcium)
1/2 multiple vitamin-mineral tablet

provides 845 kcalories, 19.9 g protein, 37.2 g fat
supports caloric needs of 28 pound dog
provides phosphorus 18%, potassium 29%, sodium 55% of a dog's daily needs.
To feed this diet with a normal amount of phosphorus substitute 4 to 5 grams bone meal powder for the 1 1/2 calcium carbonate tablets

http://dogcathomepreppareddiet.com/diet_and_chronic_renal_disease.html

## Egg White and Tapioca

Low Protein, Low phosphorus, Low Potassium, Normal Sodium

3 whites from whole chicken eggs, cooked
2 cups tapioca, cooked, (125 g dry before cooking)
1 tablespoon chicken fat (14 grams)
1 1/2 calcium carbonate tablets (600 mg calcium)
1/2 multiple vitamin-mineral tablet

provides 610 kcalories, 14.1 g protein, 13 g fat
supports caloric needs of 18 pound dog
provides phosphorus 6%, potassium 33%, sodium 269% of a dog's daily needs.
To feed this diet with a normal amount of phosphorus substitute 5 grams bone meal powder for the 1 1/2 calcium carbonate tablets

http://dogcathomepreapreddiet.com/diet_and_chronic_renal_disease.html

# Chicken and Tapioca

Low Protein, Low phosphorus, Low Potassium, Low Sodium

1/2 cup cooked chicken breast (143 grams)
2 cups tapioca, cooked, (125 g dry before cooking)
2 tablespoons chicken fat (28 grams)
1 1/2 calcium carbonate tablets (600 mg calcium)
1/2 multiple vitamin-mineral tablet

provides 763 kcalories, 20.8 g protein, 27.3 g fat
supports caloric needs of 24 to 25 pound dog
provides phosphorus 20%, potassium 22%, sodium 55% of
a dog's daily needs.
To feed this diet with a normal amount of phosphorus
substitute 5 grams bone meal powder for the 1 1/2
calcium carbonate tablets

http://dogcathomeprepareddiet.com/diet_and_chronic_r
enal_disease.html

## Eggs and Rice

Low Protein, Low phosphorus, Low Potassium, Normal Sodium

1 cooked whole egg, chicken
2 cups cooked rice, white polished, long-grain (320grams)
1 tablespoon chicken fat (14 grams)
1 1/2 calcium carbonate tablets (600 mg calcium)
1/2 multiple vitamin-mineral tablet

provides 721 kcalories, 15.2 g protein, 31.4 g fat
supports caloric needs of 23 pound dog
provides phosphorus 40%, potassium 30%, sodium 90% of a dog's daily needs.
To feed this diet with a normal amount of phosphorus substitute 3 grams bone meal powder for the 1 1/2 calcium carbonate tablets

http://dogcathomeprepareddiet.com/diet_and_chronic_renal_disease.html

## Egg White and Rice

Low Protein, Low phosphorus, Low Potassium, Normal Sodium

3 whites from whole chicken eggs, cooked
2 cups cooked rice, white polished, long-grain (320 grams)
2 tablespoons chicken fat (28 grams)
1 1/2 calcium carbonate tablets (600 mg calcium)
1/2 multiple vitamin-mineral tablet

provides 693 kcalories, 18.8 g protein, 26.8 g fat
supports caloric needs of 21 to 22 pound dog
provides phosphorus 27%, potassium 43%, sodium 208% of a dog's daily needs.
To feed this diet with a normal amount of phosphorus substitute 4 grams bone meal powder for the 1 1/2 calcium carbonate tablets

http://dogcathomeprepareddiet.com/diet_and_chronic_renal_disease.html

## Egg & Potato Diet

(low-protein, low-phosphorous, high-potassium, normal sodium)

1 egg, large, cooked
3 cups potato, boiled with skin
1 tablespoon chicken fat
1 1/2 calcium carbonate tablets (600 milligrams calcium)
1/2 mulitple-mineral tablet

Provides 600 kilocalories, 15.1 grams protein, 18.5 grams fat.Supports caloric needs of an 18-pound dogProvides phosphorus at 53 percent, potassium at 322 percent, sodium at 114 percent of dogs daily needs. To feed this diet with a normal amount of phosphorus, substitute 3 bonemeal tablets for the 1 1/2 carbonate tablets.

# Rice, Beef and Egg Diet

(Balanced low-protein, Low-phosphorus homemade formulas for adult dogs ***)

"Small Animal Clinical Nutrition, 4th edition.", Editors: Hand, Thatcher, Remillard and Roudebush et al. Making Pet Foods at Home. Topeka, KS: Mark Morris Institute, 2000, 70 authors.

(use beef with regular fat content, NOT lean beef (note S. Fleisher))

Daily food as fed formulation for a 18-kg dog

Ingredients Grams (To convert grams to ounces, multiply the grams by .0353)

Rice, white, cooked*** 237Beef, regular, cooked + 78Egg, large, boiled 20Bread, white 50Oil, vegetable 3Calcium carbonate 1.5Salt, iodized 0.5Total 390

Nutrient analysis (DM)++

Dry matter (%) 41.0Energy (kcal/l 00 g) 445Protein (%) 21.1Fat (%) 13.7Linoleic acid % 1.8Crude fiber (%)

1.4Calcium (%) 0.43Phosphorus (%) 0.22Potassium (%) 0.26Sodium (%) 0.33Magnesium 0.091

*Also feed one human adult vitamin-mineral tablet daily to dogs to ensure all vitamins and trace minerals are included. **ESHA Research. Diet Analysis Software. Food Processor Plus, version 5.03, 1990 Salem, OR. Agricultural Software Consultants, Inc. Mixit 2+, version 3.0,1991, Kingsville, TX***May substitute rice baby cereal and flavor either selection with meat broth during cooking. +Retain the fat. ++Nutrients of concern are protein, phosphorus, and potassium.

# KIDNEY HAPPY MEATLOAF

From the Kitchen of/Created by: Carolyn & Timber
**(and one of our favorites)**

1-1.5 Carrots
2 Sweet Potatoes/Yams
Any leftover veggies or misc frozen veggies (no onions)
1/2lb Kidney* Beans, cooked (or other beans) - if canned, no salt added
1.5lb Ground Turkey, Chicken, Beef, Lamb (or other meat, choose high fat)
3 Egg whites, 1 Egg yolk (keep shells, see below**)
1/4c breadcrumbs (plain or w/ spices, prefer no salt added) or Corn Flakes
1.5tsp low/no-sodium boullion cubes (veggie or any meat flavor) - ensure no onion in ingredients

Optional**: Balance your calcium to phos - add 3/4tsp crushed eggshell for every1lb or 2c of food made. Double or triple the amount to act as a phosphorus binder!

Option: Add some liver for added flavor and iron for anemic dogs. Liver is high in phos.
Option: Add kidney, which is beneficial to kidneys according to Traditional Chinese Medicine.
Do not add more than 10% organ meats to this recipe, or any CRF diet (too high in phosphorus).

## Directions

1. Heat oven to 350 F.
2. Lightly grease a loaf pan or small baking dish, OR use muffin pan for individual servings.
3. In a large bowl: shred carrots, potatoes and any leftover veggies.
4. Hand mix/mash remaining ingredients into veggie mixture until no lumps.
5. Place mixture into baking dish, spread evenly.
6. Bake for approx 45-55min (less when using muffin pans).
7. Cool.
8. Slice into desired pieces and feed - wrap individual meal sized pieces in foil or baggies and store in ziploc in freezer if desired.

# Fully Balanced Diet That Will Help With Kidney Disease

Here's a recipe for a fully balanced diet that will help with kidney disease. This comes from Small Animal Clinical Nutrition, 4th Edition (a veterinary nutrition textbook).

*Daily food as fed formulation for an 18kg (40lb) dog. Change the amounts based on the size of the dog. Food can be weighed with a regular cooking scale or other gram scale.*

Cooked white rice
(may substitute rice baby cereal and flavor with meat broth during cooking)--237g

Cooked regular beef (retain the fat)--78g

Large boiled egg--20g

White bread--50g

Vegetable oil--3g

Calcium carbonate--1.5g

Iodized salt--0.5g

1 human multivitamin

## Sticky Rice and Meat

Mix 1/2 cooked sticky rice (sushi rice) cooked in unsalted butter with 1/2 HIGH fat hamburger or dark meat chicken (lower in phosphorus than white meat).

Add two cooked egg whites (no yolk) per cup.

You can make as large a batch as needed and freeze for daily portions.

Save the egg shells, and add back one teaspoon of egg shell (dry overnight, grind in a coffee bean grinder) per two pounds of food. The egg shell is good for calcium and also acts as a phosphorus binder.

This recipe attributed to Lew Olson. PhD

## Malt O' Meal

Cook Malt o Meal and add one tablespoon of unsalted butter per cup.

Cool, and add two tablespoons of heavy whipping cream (don't need to whip it!).

You may add a bit of meat (hamburger, ground chicken) and some gravy for flavor. I have also added chicken skin or beef fat for variety.

This recipe attributed to Lew Olson. PhD

## Rice, Sweet Potato and Meat

Cook sticky rice (sushi rice) and add unsalted butter.

Mix at 1/3 sticky rice, to 1/3 boiled sweet potatoes, and add 1/3 either ground pork, lamb or fatty hamburger.

Add one egg white per cup. (You can substitute boiled potatoes for sweet potatoes).

This recipe attributed to Lew Olson. PhD

## Beef and Rice

Ingredients

¼ pound ground beef (do not use lean)
2 cups cooked white rice (no salt)
1 hard cooked egg, peeled and chopped
3 slices white bread, crumbled
1 teaspoon calcium carbonate (blend a bottle of calcium carbonate in the blender until it's a powder then keep in a resealable plastic bag)

Instructions

1. Cook the beef until it is cooked through.
2. Stir in the remaining ingredients and mix it well.
3. Feed twice a day.
4. Be sure to give your dog a vitamin supplement.

Our neighbor

## Meat and Cereal

1 cup ground meat (boiled or raw)

Chopped boiled egg

1/4 cup cooked plain oatmeal or rice

¼ cup boiled carrots

2 Tablespoons of Cottage Cheese

From a friend that runs an animal shelter

## Chicken, Egg and Rice

1 cup boiled or raw poultry, chopped

Chopped boiled egg

1/4 cup cooked brown rice

½ cup boiled mixed vegetables

2 Tablespoons of Yogurt

From a friend that runs an animal shelter

# Homecooked for Kidney Disease/ Failure

This recipe is from Dr. Pitcairn's Complete Guide to Natural Health for Dogs and Cats:

1/2 cup (1/4 lb.) regualr-fat hamburger
1 egg
2 tbl cold-pressed safflowetr, soy or corn oil
600 mg.'s calcium
1/8 tsp iodized salt
2 tbls parlsey, finely grated carrot or other veggie
1/2 -1 clove garlic minced

Dog Viatmins: (as recommended on label for a medium sized dog) 20 mg.-level B complex, 5,000 IU vitamins A, 1, 000 mg. Vitamin C (or 1/4 tsp sodium ascorbate)

Mix all ingredients and serve raw if dog will accept it. Otherwise, mix all but the vitamins and bakke in a moderate oven for 20 minutes and cool, then mix in vitamins. Be sure to provide plently of filtered water ayt all times.

Yield: Generally feed as much as your dog will eat but as a guideline this recipe should feed a 10 lb toy for 3 days or a 40 lb dog for a day. By tripling it you can feed a 60 lb dog for 3 days.
Note: If your dog isn't eating well, forcefeed vitamins separately.usinbg these daily levels: toys/ small dogs 10

mg Vit B complex & 250 mg C; medium sized dog per the recipe/ large and giant dogs 50 mg B complex and 2000 mg Vit C.

## Kidney Healing Recipe

Rudy Edalati's Barker's Grub

1 cup (8 oz) ground beef
2 tbsp olive oil
2 cups cooked white rice
1/ cup beef broth (1 1/2cups cubed or ground beef , 2
1/2 cups water, boil ground for 30 minutes, cubed for 45
min's, strain meat and reserve for another recipe)

Brown beef in oil over low heat until cooked through,
combine beef, broth and rice (should be soupy) and cool

You can substitute ground chicken or turkey for beef in
same proportions just be certain to use chicken broth for
chicken and turkey broth for turkey.

## Egg & Potato Diet

(low-protein, low-phosphorous, high-potassium, normal sodium)

1 egg, large, cooked

3 cups potato, boiled with skin

1 tablespoon chicken fat

1 1/2 calcium carbonate tablets (600 milligrams calcium)

1/2 mulitple-mineral tablet

Provides 600 kilocalories, 15.1 grams protein, 18.5 grams fat.Supports caloric needs of an 18-pound dogProvides phosphorus at 53 percent, potassium at 322 percent, sodium at 114 percent of dogs daily needs. To feed this diet with a normal amount of phosphorus, substitute 3 bonemeal tablets for the 1 1/2 carbonate tablets.

From "Home-prepared Dog and Cat Diets, The Healthful Alternative", Donald R. Strombeck, DVM, The Iowa State University Press, 2121 South State Ave., Ames Iowa 50014. 1-800-862-6657.

## Chicken and Potato diet

(low protein low phosphorus, high potassium, low sodium)

1/4 cup cooked chicken breast

3 cups potato, boiled with skin

2 tablespoons chicken fat

1 1/2 calcium carbonate tablets (600 milligrams calcium)

1/2 multiple vitamin-mineral tablet

  Provides 689 kilocalories, 18.9 grams protein, 26.8 grams fat.Supports caloric needs of a 21-22 pound dogProvides phosphorus at 45 percent, potassium at 301 percent, sodium at 54 percent of a dog's daily needs. To feed this diet with a normal amount ofphosphorus, substitute 4 bonemeal tablets for the 1 1/2 calcium carbonatetablets.

From "Home-prepared Dog and Cat Diets, The Healthful Alternative", Donald R. Strombeck, DVM, The Iowa State University Press, 2121 South State Ave., Ames Iowa 50014. 1-800-862-6657.

# Rice, Beef and Egg Diet

(use beef with regular fat content, NOT lean beef (note S. Fleisher)

(Balanced low-protein, Low-phosphorus homemade formulas for adult dogs ***)

Daily food as fed formulation for a 40 lb dog

Rice, white, cooked***

½ lb Beef, regular, cooked + 1 Egg, large, boiled

2 slices Bread, white

1.75 oz Oil, vegetable

1/3 tsp Calcium carbonate

1 tsp Salt, iodized

Nutrient analysis (DM)++

Dry matter (%) 41.0Energy (kcal/l 00 g) 445Protein (%) 21.1Fat (%) 13.7Linoleic acid % 1.8Crude fiber (%) 1.4Calcium (%) 0.43Phosphorus (%) 0.22Potassium (%) 0.26Sodium (%) 0.33Magnesium 0.091

*Also feed one human adult vitamin-mineral tablet daily to dogs to ensure all vitamins and trace minerals are included. **ESHA Research. Diet Analysis Software. Food Processor Plus, version 5.03, 1990 Salem, OR. Agricultural Software Consultants, Inc. Mixit 2+, version 3.0,1991, Kingsville, TX***May substitute rice baby cereal and flavor either selection with meat broth during cooking. +Retain the fat. ++Nutrients of concern are protein, phosphorus, and potassium.

Adapted from: "Small Animal Clinical Nutrition, 4th edition.", Editors: Hand, Thatcher, Remillard and Roudebush et al. Making Pet Foods at Home. Topeka, KS: Mark Morris Institute, 2000,

# Canine Restricted Protein Diet

This is a recipe for a homemade restricted-protein diet, similar to Hill's k/d in nutritional value and effect on compromised kidney function (the recipe comes from a sheet of such that Hill's provides for vets to give to their clients.

1/4 lb. ground beef (*do not* use lean round chuck)
2 cups cooked white rice (without salt)
1 hard-cooked egg, finely chopped
3 slices white bread, crumbled
1 teaspoon (5 grams) calcium carbonate*
(*--Calcium carbonate sources: Ground egg shells; Drug and Health food stores.)

Also add a balanced supplement which fulfills the canine MDR for all vitamins and trace minerals.

Cook beef in skillet, stirring until lightly browned. Stir in remaining ingredients and mix well. This mixture is somewhat dry and its palatability can be improved by adding a little water (not milk). Keep covered in refrigerator. Yield 1-1/4 lbs.

# Beef and Tapioca Diet

(*Low-protein, low-phosphorus, low- potassium, low-sodium*)

4 ounces lean ground beef (raw weight), cooked

2 cups tapioca, cooked (125 grams dry before cooking)

2 Tablespoons chicken fat

1.5 calcium carbonate tablets (600 milligrams calcium) (i.e. TUMS)

0.5 Multiple vitamin-mineral tablet

Provides 845 kilocalories, 19.9 grams protein, 37.2 grams fat

Supports caloric needs of a 28 pound dog

Provides phosphorus at 18%, potassium at 29%, and sodium at 55% of a dog's daily needs.  To feed this diet with a normal amount of phosphorus, substitute 5-6 bone meal tablets for the 1.5 calcium carbonate tablets

Mobile Petcare Clinic of Texas

# Egg Whites and Tapioca Diet

(*Low-protein, low-phosphorus, low- potassium, normal sodium*)

Egg whites from 3 eggs, hard boiled

2 cups tapioca, cooked (125 grams dry before cooking)

1 Tablespoon chicken fat

1.5 calcium carbonate tablets (600 milligrams calcium) (i.e. TUMS)

0.5 Multiple vitamin-mineral tablet

Provides 610 kilocalories, 14.1 grams protein, 13 grams fat

Supports caloric needs of an 18 pound dog

Provides phosphorus at 6%, potassium at 33%, and sodium at 269% of a dog's daily needs. To feed this diet with a normal amount of phosphorus, substitute 6 bone meal tablets for the 1.5 calcium carbonate tablets.

Mobile Petcare Clinic of Texas

# Chicken and Tapioca Diet

(*Low-protein, low-phosphorus, low- potassium, low-sodium*)

½ cups cooked chicken breast

2 cups tapioca cooked (125 grams dry before cooking)

2 Tablespoons chicken fat

1.5 calcium carbonate tablets (600 milligrams calcium)

½ multiple vitamin-mineral tablet

Provides 763 kilocalories, 20.8 grams protein, 27.3 grams fat

Supports caloric needs of a 24-25 pound dog

Provides phosphorus at 20%, potassium at 22%, and sodium at 55% of a dog's daily needs.  To feed this diet with a normal amount of phosphorus, substitute 5-6 bone meal tablets for the 1.5 calcium carbonate tablets.

Mobile Petcare Clinic of Texas

## Eggs and Rice Diet

(*Low-protein, low-phosphorus, low- potassium, normal sodium*)

1 egg, large, hard boiled

2 cups rice, long grain, cooked

1 Tablespoon chicken fat

1.5 calcium carbonate tablets (600 milligrams calcium)

½ multiple vitamin-mineral tablet

Provides 721 kilocalories, 15.2 grams protein, 31.4 grams fat

Supports the caloric needs of a 23 pound dog

Provides phosphorus at 40%, potassium at 30%, and sodium at 90% of a dog's daily needs.  To feed this diet with a normal amount of phosphorus, substitute 4 bone meal tablets for the 1.5 calcium carbonate tablets.

Mobile Petcare Clinic of Texas

# Egg Whites and Rice Diet

(*Low-protein, low-phosphorus, low- potassium, normal sodium*)

Egg whites from 3 eggs, large, hard boiled

2 cups rice, long grain, cooked

2 Tablespoons chicken fat

1.5 calcium carbonate tablets (600 milligrams calcium)

½ multiple vitamin-mineral tablet

Provides 693 kilocalories, 18.8 grams protein, 26.8 grams fat

Supports caloric needs of a 21-22 pound dog

Provides phosphorus at 27%, potassium at 43%, and sodium at 208% of a dog's daily needs. To feed this diet with a normal amount of phosphorus, substitute 5 bone meal tablets for the 1.5 calcium carbonate tablets.

Mobile Petcare Clinic of Texas

# Heart Healthy Recipes

## For fish lovers

Some canines simply love fish dog food. If you are looking for a great fish and rice dog food recipe, then try this fresh from the sea delight. Your dog will love the unique combination of flavors. Beef and poultry are favorites, but we felt it is a good idea to have a wide variety of tastes to suit all canine palettes. Many dogs love the flavor and consistency of this unique blend of ingredients.

Ingredients

1 cup - Broccoli frozen, chopped
2 fillet - Bass freshwater
2 tbsp - Olive oil
1 ½ cups - Brown rice cooked
10 Oz - Spinach frozen

## Directions

Cook brown rice separately. We use a pressure rice cooker because it preserves the flavor of the rice much better. Heat oven to 350 Fahrenheit. Grease a pan and place two fillets of freshwater bass on it. Bake for 15 minutes. While baking the fish, place water in small saucepan and bring to boil. Then add spinach leaves and broccoli. Boil for 2 minutes, drain and cool to room temperature. After fish is ready combine rice, fish and vegetables then add the rest of the oil and mix it well. We pulverize the meal to prevent a chance of fish bone trauma as well as to make sure that "Bonny" does not pick and choose what she eats. This recipe provides a protein to carbohydrate ratio of 1:2. This meal is also a great source of dietary fiber, protein, vitamins C, A, and K, folic acid, magnesium, phosphorus, and manganese. Multivitamin supplements are optional because this recipe is complete. This recipe will provide two daily meals for 10 pound dog.

Adapted from a recipe contributed to DoggieCook.com

## Beef, Potato and Chicken Fat Diet

Normal Protein, Minimum Sodium, High Potassium, High fat

8 ounces (raw weight) lean ground beef, cooked (228 grams)
3 cups potatoes boiled in skin (369 grams)
1 tablespoon chicken fat (14 grams)
2/3 teaspoon bone meal powder (4 grams)
1/5 tablet B complex vitamin-trace mineral (made for humans)

provides 909 kcalories, 47.8 g protein, 37.9 g fat
supports caloric needs of 31 pound dog
provides sodium 105 percent, potassium 254 percent, magnesium 212 percent of dog's needs

http://www.dogcathomepreppeddiet.com

## Beef and Potato Diet

Normal Protein, Minimum Sodium, High Potassium, Lower Fat

8 ounces (raw weight) lean ground beef, cooked (228 grams)
3 cups potatoes boiled in skin (369 grams)
2/3 teaspoon bone meal powder (4 grams)
1/5 tablet B complex vitamin-trace mineral (made for humans)

provides 792 kcalories, 47.8 g protein, 24.9 g fat
supports caloric needs of 31 pound dog
provides sodium 112 percent, potassium 262 percent, magnesium 229 percent of dog's needs

http://www.dogcathomeprepareddiet.com

## Chicken, Potato and Chicken Fat Diet

Normal Protein, Minimum Sodium, High Potassium, Low Fat

1 cup cooked chicken breast (285 grams)
3 cups potatoes boiled in skin (369 grams)
1 tablespoon chicken fat (14 grams)
2/3 teaspoon bone meal powder (4 grams)
1/5 tablet B complex vitamin-trace mineral (made for humans)

provides 735 kcalories, 49.3 g protein, 17.8 g fat
supports caloric needs of 23 to 24 pound dog
provides sodium 111 percent, potassium 267 percent, magnesium 244 percent of dog's needs

http://www.dogcathomeprepareddiet.com

## Beef, Rice and Chicken Fat Diet

Normal Protein, Minimum Sodium, Low Potassium, High fat

8 ounces (raw weight) lean ground beef, cooked (228 grams)
2 cups cooked rice, white polished, long-grain (320 grams)
1 tablespoon chicken fat (14 grams)
1/2 teaspoon bone meal powder (3 grams)
1/5 tablet B complex vitamin-trace mineral (made for humans)

provides 913 kcalories, 47.6 g protein, 37.3 g fat
supports caloric needs of 31 pound dog
provides sodium 94 percent, potassium 61 percent, magnesium 135 percent of dog's needs

http://www.dogcathomeprepareddiet.com

## Beef and Rice Diet

Normal Protein, Minimum Sodium, Low Potassium, Low fat

8 ounces (raw weight) lean ground beef, cooked (228 grams)
2 cups cooked rice, white polished, long-grain (320 grams)
1/2 teaspoon bone meal powder (3 grams)
1/5 tablet B complex vitamin-trace mineral (made for humans)

provides 796 kcalories, 47.6 g protein, 25.3 g fat
supports caloric needs of 26 pound dog
provides sodium 101 percent, potassium 65 percent, magnesium 146 percent of dog's needs

http://www.dogcathomeprepareddiet.com

## Chicken, Rice and Chicken Fat Diet

Normal Protein, Minimum Sodium, Low Potassium, Moderate Fat

1 cup cooked chicken breast (285 grams)
2 cups cooked rice, white polished, long-grain (320 grams)
1 tablespoon chicken fat (14 grams)
1/2 teaspoon bone meal powder (3 grams)
1 multiple vitamin mineral tablet

provides 739 kcalories, 49.5 g protein, 18 g fat
supports caloric needs of 23 to 24 pound dog
provides sodium 103 percent, potassium 65 percent,
magnesium 159 percent of dog's needs
add salt substitute (potassium chloride, 1/4 teaspoon) to
bring potassium to 136 percent of needs

http://www.dogcathomeprepareddiet.com

## Chicken and Rice Diet

Normal Protein, Minimum Sodium, Low Potassium, Low Fat

1 cup cooked chicken breast (285 grams)
2 cups cooked rice, white polished, long-grain (320 grams)
1/2 teaspoon bone meal powder (3 grams)
1 multiple vitamin mineral tablet

provides 624 kcalories, 49.5 g protein, 5.25 g fat
supports caloric needs of 26 pound dog
provides sodium 103 percent, potassium 56 percent,
magnesium 173 percent of dog's needs
add salt substitute (potassium chloride, 1/4 teaspoon) to
bring potassium to 147 percent of need

http://www.dogcathomeprepareddiet.com

# Seafood delight

Some pet owners neglect the benefits of seafood in their pet's diet. A seafood dog food recipe can provide many essential components to keep your pet looking and feeling healthy. A brown rice dog food is good, but may not be enough to keep your canine interested. Consider tempting your picky eater with a new seafood dog food that offers a whole new array of flavors when compared to standard chicken or beef recipes.

## Ingredients

1/2 cup - Broccoli chopped
1/2 cup - Carrots sliced
1/4 lb - Shrimps
1 large - Egg
1/4 - Mollusks, Squid, Octopus mix frozen
2 tsp - Olive oil
10 springs - Parsley raw
2 1/5 cup - Brown rice cooked

## Directions

Boil a mix of shrimps and mollusks for about 7 minutes. Chop and cook carrots for 10 minutes then add broccoli and cook for additional 5 minutes. When all ingredients are cooked through, drain excess water. Chop parsley. Mix all ingredients with cooked brown rice and add chopped, hard boiled egg. Cool to room temperature and divide in to three portions. One portion will provide nutrition for a day for a 10 pound dog. This food is a good source of protein, vitamin C, vitamin A, vitamin K, copper, selenium and manganese. Protein to carbohydrate ratio is 1:2.3 (a good ratio is 1:2 to 1:3) Multivitamins and calcium supplements need to be added. This recipe will provide three daily meals for ten pound dog.

Adapted from a recipe contributed to DoggieCook.com

## "Russian Bim"

Homemade dog food with beef and buckwheat is popular in eastern part of Europe where availability and nutritional value of buckwheat is appreciated by many dog owners.

Ingredients

½ lb of 70% Ground beef
4 cups of cooked Buckwheat
10 Oz. of cooked frozen Spinach (one package)
1/2 tsp. of Vegetable oil

Thaw frozen spinach. Cook buckwheat. We cook buckwheat in a rice cooker it helps us to keep it fresh for few days, but you can use other conventional methods if you prefer. Heat skillet and add oil and ground beef. Mix until beef is crumbly and start to changes color to brown. Add spinach to beef mix for about 2 more minutes until beef is brown. Mix buckwheat and beef and cool to room temperature before feeding. This food is a good source of protein, vitamin A, vitamin K, iron and manganese. Protein to carbohydrate ratio is 1:2. Fish oil and multivitamins can be added to balance this meal even more, but it is not absolutely necessary due to great nutritional value of ingredients. Total recipe yields three servings for a ten pound dog.

Adapted from a recipe contributed to DoggieCook.com

# Shaoping chicken

This chicken dog food recipe is a special one because it was our very first creation. We searched for a commercial dog food that our dog would enjoy. No matter what we tried, our dog refused to eat prepackaged meals. We experimented with a few combinations, such as chicken soup dog food and brown rice dog food, before finally coming up with this enticing dish. Although it lacks in a few vitamins, it is overall a well balanced homemade dog food chicken recipe and can easily be supplemented for a well rounded meal plan. Try this chicken rice dog food and see if your canine loves it as much as ours did!

## Ingredients

½ lb - Chicken dark meat
2 tsp - Olive oil
2 - Slice of bacon
2 cups - Brown rice cooked
10 Oz - Vegetables mixed frozen

## Directions

The first step is to prepare brown rice. We used a rice cooker to guarantee the perfect tenderness, but you can use more traditional methods. New crop rice is ideal for higher quality and taste benefits. Place deboned chicken and vegetables in a large sauce pan. We chose dark meat chicken over light; however this is completely up to you. Add water and stir until the mixture is smooth and well combined. Bring to a boil over medium heat, stirring constantly. Once the chicken is cooked through, drain excess liquid and add rice as well as two spoonfuls of canola oil. Stir on low heat for about one minute or until remaining water has evaporated.

As an alternative you can mix rice, chicken and veggies at the beginning and cook all together. The only disadvantage to this method is that the rice will be overcooked by the time the vegetables and chicken have finished cooking. Cool completely prior to serving. This dish can be stored in the refrigerator. Add a high quality multivitamins and for canines over five years of age, also add one capsule of fish oil.

Adapted from a recipe contributed to DoggieCook.com

# Veggie lamb

Some canines may be adventurous eaters, but also may have an allergy to beef. Why not add something new to your dog's diet that is a proven favorite among canine taste testers? Many commercial foods offer lamb and rice dog food varieties. While these may be flavorful, a homemade lamb and rice dog food will be a pure treat for your pet. This is a great dish for pet owners who have time to prepare their dog's meal. The simple components and great taste that go into this one have been approved by our dog, "Minkey". Lamb is also known to be hypoallergenic and good source of protein.

## Ingredients

1 cup – Broccoli frozen chopped
1 – Carrot
1 cup – Cauliflower frozen chopped
½ lb - Lamb ground
1 tsp – Corn oil
2 ½ cup – Rice white

## Directions

Cook rice. We cook rice in a rice cooker to keep it fresh and flavorful, but you can use other conventional methods if you prefer. Chop carrots in to small pieces (about 1/2 inch). Boil broccoli, carrots and cauliflower together for 5 minutes. Heat skillet and add oil and ground lamb. Mix until lamb is crumbly and changes color to brown. Add vegetables to lamb and rice. Cool to room temperature before feeding. This food is a good source of protein, vitamin A, vitamin C, vitamin K and manganese. Protein to carbohydrate ratio is 1:2. Fish oil and multivitamins need to be added to balance out the meal. Total recipe yields three servings for a nine pound dog.

Adapted from a recipe contributed to DoggieCook.com

## Beef and Potato Diet

(Normal Protein, high-potassium, minimum sodium, moderate fat)

8 ounces lean ground beef (raw weight), cooked (for best results, **boil** ground beef and pour off water and fat)

3 cups potato, boiled with skin

5 bonemeal tablets (10-grain or equivalent) – OR – 1-1/4 teaspoons of bonemeal powder

1 multiple vitamin-mineral tablet

Provides 792 kilocalories, 27.8 grams protein, 24.9 grams fat
Supports caloric needs of a 26-pound dog
Provides sodium at 112 percent, potassium at 262 percent, magnesium at 229 percent of a dog's daily needs

http://bigheartsfund.org

## Chicken and Potato Diet
(Normal Protein, high-potassium, minimum sodium, low-fat)

1 cup cooked chicken breast

3 cups potato, boiled with skin

4 bonemeal tablets (10-grain or equivalent) – OR- 1 teaspoon bonemeal powder

1 multiple vitamin mineral tablet

http://bigheartsfund.org

## Beef and Rice Diet

(Normal protein, low-potassium, minimum sodium, moderate fat)

8 ounces lean ground beef (raw weight), cooked (for best results, boil ground beef and pour off fat and water)

2 cups rice, long-grain, cooked

4 bonemeal tablets – OR – 1 teaspoon bonemeal powder

1 multiple vitamin mineral tablet

Provides 796 kilocalories, 47.6 grams protein, 25.3 grams fat
Supports caloric needs of a 26-pound dog
Provides sodium at 101 percent, potassium at 65 percent, magnesium at 146 percent of a dog's daily needs
Add salt substitute (potassium chloride, 1/4 teaspoon) to bring potassium to 147 percent of needs.

http://bigheartsfund.org

## Chicken and Rice Diet

(Normal protein, low potassium, minimum sodium, low fat)

1 cup cooked chicken breast

2 cups rice, long-grain, cooked

4 bonemeal tablets – OR – 1 teaspoon bonemeal powder

1 multiple vitamin mineral tablet

Provides 624 kilocalories, 49.5 grams protein, 5.25 grams fat
Supports caloric needs of a 26-pound dog
Provides sodium at 103 percent, potassium at 56 percent, magnesium at 173 percent or a dog's daily needs
Add salt substitute (potassium chloride, 1/4 teaspoon) to bring potassium to 147 percent of needs.

http://bigheartsfund.org

## Heart Healthy Chicken

4 Cups Cubed cooked boneless skinless chicken breast
3 Cups Cooked long-grain brown rice
2 1/4 Cups Pureed fruit and vegetables (minimum, please
feel free to increase fruits and veg)
2 Tablespoons *Oil Blend
Add a dose of Dog Greens to each meal as recommended
in daily program schedule immediately before serving.

Five Leaf Pet Pharmacy

# Healthy Treats

## Turkey Dog Treats

From Thrifty Fun

Ingredients:

- 1 lb. of cooked turkey blended ( NO turkey skin, bones, or fat)
- 2 eggs
- 3 cups of flour
- 1 cup quick cooking rolled oats
- 1 cup water or broth*

**Note:** If using broth remember that onions and garlic (raw, cooked, or powder) are harmful to dogs so it's suggested not to use it! (in the original recipe)

Directions:

In a blender or food processor, combine turkey meat and beaten eggs until well blended and set aside.

In a large bowl, combine flour and rolled oats and add blended turkey. Add water or broth to flour, stir till dough is sticky.

Divide dough into 2 balls. Knead each ball on a well floured surface (about 2 minutes), adding flour until the dough is no longer sticky.

With a rolling pin, roll out dough to between 1/4 to 1/2 inch thickness. Cut with biscuit cutter and place on lightly greased baking sheet.

Bake 1 hour at 350 degrees F (180 degrees C). Time should adjusted if size is different than in this recipe.

Cool on rack and store, at room temperature, in a container with loose fitting lid.

They should keep for 3 weeks, however you can freeze for longer use.

Source: Recipe is from Mac Pherson's K-9 Cookbook. I substituted turkey in the place of ground beef.

## Albi's Treats

The treat recipe is from Brad Luther. He and his veterinarian made the recipe for Brad's Boxer, Albi.

I have adapted these ingredients to meet Albi's needs. there are many healthy ingredients other dogs can eat but because of her situation this recipe is limited. With input from the vet, these ingredients have been chosen for easy processing by the kidneys.

Albi's treats:

- 2 1/2 cups whole wheat flour
- 1/2 tsp. garlic powder
- 6 Tblsps. low sodium, low fat chicken broth
- 1/2 cup cold water1 cup cooked vegetable (green beans, carrots or mixed)

Combine flour and garlic powder. Mix in chicken broth and vegetable(s).add enough cold water to form a ball. Pat dough to 1/2" and cut with a dog biscuit cutter, cookie cutter or knife. Place on a non-stick cookie sheet & bake in a preheated oven @ 350F for 25 minutes. Cool on a wire rack. Since there are no preservatives, I recommend storing them in the refrigerator if they are not eaten within a week. They can also be made ahead and frozen.

# Peanut Butter Cookies

*Our dogs love these and the neighbor's dog loves them as well.*

Dogs love peanut butter, and these cookies are a great way to sneak some fish oil into your dog's diet. Fish oil improves your dog's coat, making it shiny, soft, and healthier.

Look for organic peanut butter at your grocery store. Many commercial brands of peanut butter have unhealthy hydrogenated oils and additives. Better yet, make your own peanut butter using raw peanuts and peanut oil, and processing the mixture in your food processor.

Ingredients

2 cups of flour (white or wheat, if your pup has no wheat allergies)
1 cup of rolled oats
1/3 cup of smooth peanut butter
1 tablespoon of honey
1/2 tablespoon of fish oil
1 1/2 cups of water

## Directions

1. Preheat the oven to 350 degrees Fahrenheit.
2. Mix the flour and oats together in a large mixing bowl. Pour in one cup of water and blend until smooth. Add in the peanut butter, honey, and fish oil and mix until all the ingredients are well blended.
3. Slowly add the water until the mixture has a thick and doughy consistency.
4. Lightly flour a cooking surface. Roll the dough onto the cooking surface to create a 1/4 inch thick sheet.
5. Use a cookie cutter to create shapes. Place the cookies onto a baking sheet and bake for 40 minutes.
6. Allow to cool completely before feeding.

*Pro Tip*: If the dough is too sticky to roll, slowly pad more flour onto the dough ball.

From Money Crashers

## Chicken Jerky

The jerky is tough and chewy, so it keeps a dog occupied for a while, and the chicken has a good amount of protein, which is good for a dog's muscle structure.

Ingredients

2 to 4 chicken breasts

Directions

1. Preheat the oven to 200 degrees Fahrenheit.
2. Remove any excess fat from the chicken. Turn the chicken breast on its side and use a paring knife to slice the chicken breast into 1/8 inch thick strips.
3. Set the strips on a baking sheet. Bake for 2 hours.
4. Check the chicken before removing from the oven. It should be dry and hard, not soft or chewy. Allow the chicken to cool completely before serving.
5. Store the jerky in an airtight container in the fridge for up to two weeks.

*Pro Tip*: You can substitute sweet potatoes for the chicken in this recipe. Sweet potatoes make a healthy, vegetarian alternative.

From Money Crashers

# Fruit and Vegetable Strips

These strips work as a cheaper alternative to the organic chewy treats sold in pet stores. They also break apart easily, so you can serve smaller pieces as training rewards. Fruits and vegetables are rich in vitamin C, which can help boost your dog's immune system.

## Ingredients

- 1 small sweet potato
- 1 medium banana
- 1 cup carrots, minced
- 1/2 cup unsweetened organic applesauce
- 2 cups of whole wheat flour (white if your dog has allergies)
- 1 cup of rolled oats
- 1/3 cup of water

## Directions

1. Cook the sweet potato in the microwave for 8 to 10 minutes, or until the insides are soft. Set aside and allow to cool.
2. Preheat the oven to 350 degrees Fahrenheit.
3. Mash the banana and sweet potato in a large mixing bowl with a hand masher until smooth. Add in the

carrots, flour, and oats. Slowly add in the applesauce and water while mixing.

4. The ingredients will form a soft dough. Roll the dough on to a lightly floured surface until the dough is 1/8 inch thick.
5. Cut the dough into strips.
6. Cook on a baking sheet for 25 minutes.
7. Store leftover strips in the fridge for up to two weeks.

*Pro Tip*: Do not worry about overcooking the sweet potato. Softer potatoes will mash easier.

From Money Crashers

# Vegan Dog Food Recipes

I have been asked to include these recipes for people who
have pets that have special dietary needs such as meat
allergies or for those that do not wish for their four-legged
friend to consume animal protein.

# Homemade Sweet-Potato Peanut-Butter Vegan-Dog Delight

6 cups (filtered) water

1 cup mixed rice and quinoa (I mix black, brown, and long grain rice with black and/or
white quinoa.)

1 cup mixed lentils (I mix green, red, and French lentils.)

3 medium sweet potatoes sliced into 1-inch cubes

3 cups or 24 oz. natural peanut butter

1&frac12; cups or 8 to 12-oz. apple cider vinegar, optional (My dog is a flat-nosed breed, which means she tends to get gassy. The vinegar gets rid of virtually all of her gas, but if your dog does not have a problem with this, you can omit the vinegar.)

8 g hemp protein

1 Tbsp. flaxseed oil with DHA (Store in the fridge or freezer.)

200-250 mg cranberry extract (Since a vegan diet is alkalizing, your dog may need this acidifier to maintain a healthy urinary pH.)

VegeDog multivitamin powder

Prozyme Plus (This helps with digestion so that your dog

can absorb as many nutrients as possible.)
125 mg PB8 brand probiotic (1/4 pill)

Boil the water.
Add the rice, lentils, and sweet potatoes.
Reduce the heat and simmer, covered, for 40 minutes to 1 hour, or until all ingredients are soft. Stir occasionally and add more water as needed. Too much water is better than not enough water. (Remember, you want the ingredients to be extra moist because they will be easier to digest.)

Mash the sweet potatoes with a fork and mix thoroughly. Let cool.
Add the peanut butter and vinegar. Stir well.
Place 3 to 5 servings in your refrigerator and store the rest in the freezer.
Measure 2/3 cup of food per meal.*

At mealtime: Add hemp protein, flaxseed oil, cranberry extract, Vegedog, Prozyme Plus, and PB8 into the 2/3 cup of food. Mix well and serve twice daily.

* Serving size is based on the diet of a 20-lb. dog. Please adjust the portion size to suit your dog's weight.

peta.org via Corinne Alexaki

# Vegetable Stew

## Ingredients

3 tbsp. olive oil
3 garlic cloves, crushed
1 large pepper (sweet, not hot), sliced
1 medium zucchini, sliced
1 medium yellow squash, sliced
1 medium Eggplants, peeled & cubed
1 Potato, peeled & cubed
1 tsp. oregano or basil
salt/pepper

## Directions

Heat oil; add garlic and saute for 2-3 minutes until softened. Add all of the vegetables. Mix thoroughly. Bring the mixture to a boil, then lower the heat and let simmer for 30 minutes. Add the seasonings to taste. Simmer 15 minutes more. Let cool. Top with grated Cheese, if desired.

Organic-pet-digest.com

## Veggie Vittles

Ingredients

1 egg, beaten
1/3 cup applesauce
1 cup cooked vegetables*, mashed or grated small
1 cup cooked rice
1 tbsp. brewers yeast
*Any desired veggies can be used, such as zucchini, Peas,
carrots, potatoes, etc... Directions

Mix all ingredients well. Drop by rounded teaspoonfuls
onto a greased cookie sheet.  Bake in a preheated 350
degree oven for about 12 minutes, or until lightly browned
and firm. Cool. Store in the fridge, or freeze.

Organic-pet-digest.com

# Vegan Dog Treats

## Voo Doo Bones

### Ingredients

3 cups minced parsley
1/4 cup carrots, chopped very fine
2 tablespoons olive oil
2 3/4 cups whole wheat flour
2 tablespoons bran
2 teaspoons baking powder
1/2 to 1 cup of water

### Directions

Preheat oven to 350 degrees, rack on middle level. Lightly grease a large baking sheet. Stir together parsley, carrots and oil. Combine all the dry ingredients and add to veggies. Gradually add 1/2 cup of water, mixing well. Make a moist but not wet dough. If needed, add a little more water. Knead for one minute. Roll dough out to 1/2 inch thickness. Using cookie cutter or a glass, cut out the shapes and transfer them to the baking sheet. Gather the scraps and reroll and cut. Bake for 20-30 minutes until biscuits have browned and hardened slightly. (They will harden more as they cool.) Speed cooling by placing them on wire racks. Store in airtight tin.

Organic-pet-digest.com

# Oatmeal Wheat Dog Biscuit Treats

## Ingredients

1 cup uncooked oatmeal
1 tablespoon bouillon* granules (Beef, Chicken or vegetable)
1 egg, beaten
1 1/2 cups hot water
3/4 cups cornmeal 3 cups whole wheat flour

## Directions

Preheat oven to 325 F. In a large bowl pour hot water over oatmeal and bouillon granules: let stand 5 minutes. Stir in cornmeal and egg. Add flour, 1/2 cup at a time, mixing well after each addition. Knead 3 to 4 minutes, adding more flour if necessary to make a very stiff dough. Pat or roll dough to 1/2 inch thickness. Cut into bone shapes and place on a greased baking sheet. Bake for 50 minutes. Allow to cool and dry out until hard. Makes approximately 1 3/4 pounds. Store in an airtight container Organic-pet-digest.com

# Doggie Biscuits

## Ingredients

1/2 cup shortening
3 Tbsp. honey
4 eggs
1 tsp. vanilla
1 cup whole wheat flour
1/4 cup carob powder
1/2 tsp. baking powder

## Directions

Cream shortening and honey together thoroughly. Add remaining ingredients. Beat well. Bake in a greased cookie sheet (10x15") for 25 minutes at 350 degrees. Cool completely.

Organic-pet-digest.com

# Can Recipes Be Copyrighted?

I included this section so that you can read about the legalities of sharing these recipes. I encourage you to share them with anyone who has a four legged family member who is suffering and is in need of dietary help. You may reduce suffering and extend the life of someone's beloved pet.

Via Kottke, a <u>Washington Post article on protection of recipes</u>
One should distinguish between a recipe, a textual rendering of a recipe, and a compilation of recipes. Publications Intl. v. Meredith, 88 F.3d 473 (7th Cir. 1996) dealt with alleged infringement of a recipe book:
"The identification of ingredients necessary for the preparation of each dish is a statement of facts. There is no expressive element in each listing; in other words, the author who wrote down the ingredients for "Curried Turkey and Peanut Salad" was not giving literary expression to his individual creative labors. Instead, he was writing down an idea, namely, the ingredients necessary to the preparation of a particular dish. "[N]o author may copyright facts or ideas. The copyright is limited to those aspects of the work—termed 'expression'—that display the stamp of the author's originality." Harper & Row, 471 U.S. at 547, 105 S.Ct. at 2223. We do not view the functional listing of ingredients as original within the meaning of the Copyright Act.

Nor does Meredith's compilation copyright in DISCOVER DANNON extend to facts contained within that compilation. As the Supreme Court stated in Feist: Facts, whether alone or as part of a compilation, are not original and therefore may not be copyrighted. A factual compilation is eligible for copyright if it features an original selection or arrangement of facts, but the copyright is limited to the particular selection or arrangement. In no event may copyrights extend to the facts themselves. Feist, 499 U.S. at 350-51, 111 S.Ct. at 1290. The lists of ingredients lack the requisite element of originality and are without the scope of copyright. The Copyright Office itself has stated that "mere listing[s] of ingredients or contents" are not copyrightable. 37 C.F.R. s 202.1. The next question is whether the directions for combining these ingredients may warrant copyright protection. The DISCOVER DANNON recipes' directions for preparing the assorted dishes fall squarely within the class of subject matter specifically excluded from copyright protection by 17 U.S.C. s 102(b). Webster's defines a recipe as: a set of instructions for making something ... a formula for cooking or preparing something to be eaten or drunk: a list of ingredients and a statement of the procedure to be followed in making an item of food or drink ... a method of procedure for doing or attaining something. WEBSTER'S THIRD NEW INTERNATIONAL DICTIONARY (Merriam-Webster 1986). The recipes at issue here describe a procedure by which the reader may produce many dishes featuring Dannon yogurt. As such, they are excluded from copyright protection as either a "procedure, process, [or] system." 17 U.S.C. s 102(b).

Meredith fashioned processes for producing appetizers, salads, entrees, and desserts. Although the inventions of "Swiss 'n' Cheddar Cheeseballs" and "Mediterranean Meatball Salad" were at some time original, there can be no monopoly in the copyright sense in the ideas for producing certain foodstuffs.

Nor can there be copyright in the method one might use in preparing and combining the necessary ingredients. Protection for ideas or processes is the purview of patent. The order and manner in which Meredith presents the recipes are part and parcel of the copyright in the compilation, but that is as far as it goes. As Professor Nimmer states: This conclusion [i.e., that recipes are copyrightable] seems doubtful because the content of recipes are clearly dictated by functional considerations, and therefore may be said to lack the required element of originality, even though the combination of ingredients contained in the recipes may be original in a noncopyright sense. 1 MELVILLE B. NIMMER & DAVID NIMMER, NIMMER ON COPYRIGHT s 2.18[I], at 2- 204.25-.26 (May 1996)."

Made in the USA
Las Vegas, NV
11 September 2024

94979256R10052